IN DOCTOR NO'S GARDEN

For Matt,

With good wishes,

Henry Hall

St John's College
Feb '08

IN DOCTOR NO'S GARDEN

GARDEN

Henry Shukman

CAPE POETRY

Published by Jonathan Cape 2002

4 6 8 10 9 7

First published in Great Britain in 2002 by
Jonathan Cape
Random House, 20 Vauxhall Bridge Road,
London SW1V 2SA

Random House Australia (Pty) Limited
20 Alfred Street, Milsons Point, Sydney,
New South Wales 2061, Australia

Random House New Zealand Limited
18 Poland Road, Glenfield
Auckland 10, New Zealand

Random House South Africa (Pty) Limited
Endulini, 5A Jubilee Road, Parktown 2193, South Africa

The Random House Group Limited Reg. No. 954009
www.randomhouse.co.uk

A CIP catalogue record for this book
is available from the British Library

ISBN 0-224-06913-6

Papers used by Random House are natural,
recyclable products made from wood grown in sustainable forests;
the manufacturing processes conform to the environmental
regulations of the country of origin.

Typeset by Palimpsest Book Production Limited,
Polmont, Stirlingshire
Printed and bound in Great Britain by
Biddles Ltd, King's Lynn, Norfolk

for Clare

CONTENTS

ACKNOWLEDGEMENTS

Acknowledgements are due to the editors of the following:

Arvon Journal, Birmingham Post, boomeranguk.com, Cornucopia, Cream City Review, Daily Telegraph, Daily Telegraph Arvon Prize Anthology 2000, Exeter Prize Poems 1998, Forward Book of Poetry 2002, Harvard Review, Hudson Review, Iowa Review, London Magazine, London Review of Books, New Forest Prize Anthology 2000, New Mexican, North American Review, Peterloo Prize Anthology 2000, The Rialto, Sin Fronteras Journal, Stand, Tabla Book of New Verse 2000 and *2001, The Times Literary Supplement*

'Scientists' won second prize in the 2000 *Times Literary Supplement*/Blackwells Poetry Competition; 'Ararat' won first prize in the 2000 *Daily Telegraph* Arvon Poetry Competition; 'Piano Solo' won first prize in the 2000 *Tabla* Poetry Competition and was shortlisted for the 2001 Forward Prize for Best Single Poem; 'Snowy Morning' was a prizewinner in the 2000 Peterloo Poetry Competition (under the title 'Frosty Morning'); 'Trumpeters' won second prize in the 2001 Wells Festival Poetry Competition; 'The Ferryman' won first prize in the 2001 New Forest Poetry Competition (under the title 'River Ferry'); 'Thread' was a finalist in the 1998 Exeter Poetry Prize.

Special thanks to Keiren Phelan at Southern Arts for a timely and generous award that enabled me to complete the manuscript; also to the Arts Council of England, who I hope will forgive my using some of their award for fiction on this book. Thanks to Hawthornden Castle for a Fellowship there, and to Middlebury College, Vermont, for a Bread Loaf Scholarship.

I have been fortunate in my readers: Douglas Dunn, to whom I owe much, Sam Willetts, Tony Hoagland, Joe Somoza, Jeremy Treglown, Ian Tromp, Andy Brown, Jay Ramsay, Miriam Obrey, Maggie O'Farrell, Mark Haworth-Booth and K. West. Thanks to all; and especially to Neil Rollinson, friend, coach, critic, who trawled through the manuscript time and again. Robin Robertson's editing was inspiring and astute. For the record, thanks to Mr Meredith and Mr Moran, who will have long forgotten me. Finally, for patience and perspicacity, thanks to Clare.

MAN PEEING

My father was a man of small stature
but some standing. *Important*
in some circles, he told me,
pushing his glasses up his nose.
Which way to the Gents?
he would ask the maitre d'.
We'd place ourselves side by side
before the high white wall.
When he started to urinate
my father let out an arse-squeal.
He would laugh and I would laugh.
He was warm to the touch.
Clouds of steam rose from his pale stream.
His thing was heavy and thick,
a length of rope, a long toadstool,
a mushroom-nozzle emitting a twirled bore,
a fireman's jet. When I saw it
I understood he was of another world.
He would choose a spot and obliterate it.
Afterwards, when he zipped it away,
the zip said, *Uh-huh* in agreement.
Come on, boychick. Ready?
Full to my chin with delight
I'd nod because I was ready.
I followed him past the swinging doors
that chuckled behind us
back to the carpeted world
where the waiters and the women waited.

THREAD

Before my loose button taps to the floor, sinks in a rug,
I find my hotel mending kit, Swiss Army knife.
What would my grandfather think, the one I never knew,
the tailor, who glided out of war up a still, grey Thames,
saw the fog lift on the brick-black face of Wapping?

1910: hats and bulky overcoats, a threat
of rain, a reek of yeast, gulls truant overhead.
He running-stitched, hemmed and collared his way
from Shelter to a Shoreditch flat, then Soho, a mile north
of Savile Row, and finally a real house up Finchley Road.
Jews were always middle class, just not allowed to be.

I settle under my desk lamp, open the card,
unravel its tangled blue, then suck and find the eye.
His son's son, a middle-class boy (he got me there)
who never sat cross-legged on a table or learnt chalk's
code on cloth, never trimmed a weightless astrakhan.

His favourite work was furs. He'd unlock the chest
(the key on a neck-chain) and rifle the silent scraps –
fox and ermine, rabbit and bear – then turn a collar
with his black shears, humming, half-listening
to the city surf of whistles, wheels and cries.

I prod and pull my double thread. One bath a week –
did he smell? A grimy neck? An animal breath
of Polish sausage and tea with blackberry jam?
And what's left of him in me, a soft-skinned man
who doesn't sing or fast or pray, who bears only
the lost Yiddish scrawled on chest and shoulder?

My grandfather tuts. He taps my final inch of thread,
too short to tie a knot. *Leave that to me, you've better
things to do.* His eyebrows are thicker than I thought,
his breath fainter. His big-nailed fingers, strong as a fiddler's,
undo my work, dive and twist. His needle a dorsal glint
in water. A quick bite: done. Thread to last a lifetime.

In our little house Creedence were singing
about the old cotton fields, the baby
was flat on his back in front of the fire,
eyes swimming with flame.
Christmas morning, and you were at church.
I thought of going to join you late,
but instead took the baby up to the horses.
Out in the field he started crying.
Maybe I should have taken him to the bath
of stone, the discipline of a saviour, the sanctuary
of hymns –

But the horses saved us.
To be close to them, so tough and nothing
to do with us, and their breathing all over him,
and the flaking mud on their necks
where they had rolled, and the sucking of hooves
as they walked the sodden field.
The horses with their long heads,
underwater eyes, watched us watch them.
Then they turned, drumming the field,
leaving us alone – the damp morning
all about, the soaked grass under foot,
the baby's diaphanous ears going pink in the cold
as silence bowed back to earth.

ON EXPENSES

In the evening all over the city, table
cloths wait, smooth as meadows at dusk.
Smoke curls round your tongue because
why not chainsmoke when the Semillon
and Cassis are bathing your throat.
Soon you'll be cutting open the juices
of a grilled mignon, slicing into heavy
morelles, inhaling the fragrance of truffles.
Later when red circles have stamped
the white cloth, you'll fold the pink slip
in your wallet and congratulate yourself
on the tip that broke three figures.
In the gentle dazzle of the city's morning,
while waiters hose their terraces,
you'll dip the day's news in French
coffee, eat up the early notices
and glide all the way to lunch and beyond
on a rising tide of someone else's money.

HAPPY HARADA

Most erratic member of the Japanese Winter Olympic team,
Harada had the best and worst scores of the Nagano Games.

It's Happy Harada on the bench now.
Four years he's been waiting for this jump.
Harada pulls down his giant goggles and grins.
He stands, releasing himself, sinks
into the silver crouch, arms swept back like fins.
The skis scuffle in their grooves like cutlery
in a drawer, the wind presses against him,
flattening the smile into his face.
He hits the ramp. *Yes, it's a big take-off,*
he's certainly found a cushion this time,
oh he's flying. The skis a perfect V,
the puffed aerofoils of his sleeves. Happy
passes all the lines of the landing slope.
A hum goes round the crowd.
How's he going to bring this one down?
Telemark won't do it from that height.
But he isn't coming down. Up Happy goes,
high above the crowd, who turn up their faces
like a field of poppies, all the little flags
drooping in awe as Happy Harada soars
right over them, clean out of the arena.
Well, what will the judges make of that?
Just look at Nikkinen the Finn
shaking his head, he can't believe it.
Happy is flying, flying high over Nagano,
past the sushi places, there goes the cement
factory far below, a cloud skits by
just under his skis, he can almost taste it.
A distant ambulance wails among hills.
Happy watches as all the swallows of Nagano

flock up to meet him. They lead him off
over the temples of Mount Hiei
ducking and whistling like dolphins.

When at midnight my wife turns the shield
of her back to me, feeds the baby, then whispers,
It's OK, shh, there's another one, it's OK,
as she lifts him on her shoulder a moment
before giving him to the other breast,
I can see his face up there dark from sleep.
The eyes glisten. More than that,
they shine with their own electricity
like some feat of marine chemistry:
phosphorescence, the lambency at night
of certain polyps, an urgent bio-luminescence
with its own laws, its own necessities –
things more important than my own sleepy head
already in its prime, restless on the pillow.

PIANO SOLO

Years after my mother chose emptiness
at night I'd hear her at the piano
planting chords, waiting for them
to grow into something.

She never advanced from childhood
lessons. She'd crackle flat a dry page
of Bartok or *Anna Magdalena*
and make the house's spine go cold.

That was all her hesitant handfuls
conjured – misery, a lonely beginner
always beginning again, a weather
of notes I wished would pass.

They trickled onto my sheets
in the dark, each drop telling
how sad a woman could feel
even to have lost what made her sad.

SCHMALTZ

Chicken soup is magic, here's the proof.
Maybe if I'd opened the window a crack
it never would have happened. But late
in the war, I tip the lid to let the steam off

while the broth reduces to clear gold.
Here's my stove up one end and on the table
at the other there's the new baby, the seventh,
the one we didn't want but he was a boy,

after six girls you don't complain.
There's no place for a baby like a warm kitchen,
plus he's wrapped in my husband's
army coat, a proper little bundle.

The Germans find our house by mistake,
drop one right through the roof.
It's the new kind that drips and where it drips
it burns. The girls are all up the road thank god

at their auntie's. I dash into the kitchen,
find a sight. Shouldn't have left the stove,
is my first thought. The room's that smoky
I didn't see the fire was up the other end.

Put my hand straight in the flame.
There he is, snug in his basket, snug all right,
not a squeak or whimper from him,
I don't stop to think what that means.

I pull him out and make for the door.
Outside, I hold him away to get a look
and my whole front's stained with grease.
I wipe his cheek, the skin smooth as ever.

Even with our house pouring smoke behind me,
a tower of flame roaring from the roof,
I can smell what it is on him: schmaltz.
While the room filled with fire he'd been anointed,

and it saved him. No one explained it.
Even the doctor couldn't understand.
He's a plump man our Ruby, always has been,
and loves a bowl of chicken soup with matzoh,

I get some ready whenever he comes.
Oh mom, he says, not chicken soup again;
he's only joking. Yes it is, you ought to know
what's good for you. He's an accountant,

offices off Regent's Park, drives a BMW
just like half his sisters, the ones that didn't
throw themselves away. Wanted to be a fireman
but wasn't tall enough. Changed his name though.

Cohen to Owen. Says it helps in today's Britain.
I'm running out of breath, all this talking,
what I'm saying is, I had a miracle in my life,
never underestimate a good bowl of soup.

Friday morning we put in to Poole harbour
sea like satin sun tearing a hole in clouds
scattering rice grains the gantries like daffodils
white cottage of the Fisherman's Museum
boats on the wharf getting made up
all day unloading hake then tea and cockles
cup of pickle cup of kettle
red bus up the hill past the Royal Winchester
the Golden Finger Frying Friday and Every Day
and breath-clouds exhaust-clouds
five o'clock and the rug was down
so in we go to O'Halloran's
for the first of a fair convention
but what were we there for in they come
mine's a beauty not twenty-four
eyes of coke a mane to match
no match for us we had her and the others
talked down in minutes
in we start she and I with the jokes
I'm hearing raven's wings who is she
what is she who made her
those crude-oil eyes cheeks like a beach
I say let me buy you a dinner you won't forget
this after an eight-day trip you understand
the pockets bulging she says I don't trust a sailor
I say a fisherman isn't a sailor
she says any man that sails is a sailor
I say but we don't sail we trawl
that's why I'm a trawlerman
she's on my arm out the door
Rachel or Naomi dusky nubile of the desert
we're treading the margin of the Book
downtown at Jacksons we break

duck neck bottle neck she flies at the dance
me thinking my rainy days are over
it was not midnight when my intentions
earned their first kiss there you have it
six hours to a bride twenty-six years to follow
all good things begin on Friday
Friday has the goodwill of the world in it

From the shop comes a hum that stutters,
breaks into a roar. I pause in my scrubbing.
It could be the Piper Navajo, one of its two
big engines just trucked in from Illinois.

In the corridor a stench of ablution hangs in the dark.
A snort, a cough from a manifold, a second hum
skips to a high note, joining the first:
the Navajo for sure, both engines in business.

There'll be ten minutes of magneto checks,
just time to finish the Ladies. A nasty speckle
encrusted on the enamel takes a lot of going over.
I pour on brown caustic. That helps.

I spray the mirror and basin, wipe them down,
give the taps a rub, then wheel out my yellow bucket
of brushes, cloths, detergents. I polish the plaques
of the little man, little woman and wheelchair.

I'm happy. They may be toilets but they're mine.
Push out two stiff doors and you're on
the open plain of the ramp. A field of concrete
stretches to mountains. The sickly smell of AvGas

hangs in the air. Tomahawks and Cessnas growl
and purr as they come in for their touch-and-goes.
And from the hangar, right now, the twin-engine
Navajo shakes onto the ramp, its engines humming.

Sounds like an old war bird, says Jim the redfaced
trainee A & P. Rae leaves her typewriter. *I swore
they'd never get it out of the shop*. Even Cy the boss
breaks off his phone calls. *Nice, guys, nice.*

The four of us stand under the milky airport sky
as the plane drones down the runway. It spends
a long time turning, until the landing light glares
in our faces. *Go, Billy, go*, Cy mutters.

Billy the pilot, as if he hears, opens it out
in a straight sprint, lifts the nose off the ground,
hangs above the tarmac like a fighter plane
before folding up the wheels and banking

towards Charlotte and the flanks of Mount Morecroft.
The plane becomes a speck travelling over green hills
but we can still hear it throbbing in the distance.
I go back to tackle the Mens. As I let the flush go

there's a rattle in the ventilation, then a roar,
a deep rumble: Billy coming back fast and low,
buzzing us all. I can't imagine any place
ever feeling so much like home.

THE CRY

A cold night, but we've left the restaurant
because he wants to be walked – my son
buttoned against me in my jacket,
eyes screwed tight and leaking,
face crunched in a cry that won't stop,
that has me knee-deep in the pavement.
We pass a pub window lined with glasses,
someone's laughing inside. The cry
goes on. Outside the synagogue now,
all locked up, a motion-triggered light
flicks on. This isn't meant to be symbolic
but the moment doesn't escape me:
the two of us born outside the gates,
he wailing. His breath stutters, re-enters
the cry as if he knows: no prayerhouse,
no candles lighting the way, no wine
to sluice the passage of weeks.
But at last the milky lids come down.
He's come a long way, has a long way to go.

END OF AN ERA

The bath spills as his stomach breaks the surface:
a landmass forested with foam. The bourbon-and-branches
have silted his jaw, the martinis have made a Michelin
of his middle. 9.44 a.m. No need to shift.

He raises a soapy A–OK to his lips, sighs a stream
of bubbles – tiny O's. He adds more hot with his toes.
Out to pasture. Always thought he'd relish his days on the links,
a tear down the lanes in the E-type, dinner at Whites.

A cold shower, a suck of fierce coffee – anything
to get the wool out of his head. *O, Q or M, send me
to Siberia, get me out of suburbia before I die.
Give me a make-over, new passport, the lot.*

If only the Union hadn't snipered Tracy in the Alps.
None of the others was worth giving up the rest for.
He'll ransack the yellow pages later: *Escort, Massage.*
He might have thirty years left. A long time to kill.

Too long. One of these days: datura from Dr No's garden,
a single silver bullet from the PPK, faithful to the last,
or something shocking in the bath: *Do unplug the hairdrier
before you pull me out. Regards, Double O Out.*

LIFTER

Maria of the Carrara-Cinzano eyes,
kohled lashes and feather stole,
trails threads from her Balenciaga.
She slips into the changing room
with a chemise, a négligé of gauze,
a silk nightie, and pulls them all on.
Her fingers tremble on her coat buttons.
She drifts to the underwear racks
and fills her pockets with lace.
Her Pucci pumps are beyond cleaning,
the heels are gone, but she glides
out the door like a deposed princess
who has to live in a walk-up,
which is just what she is.

he gave me was no accident. The last face
he saw was mine. Sometimes I think of him
sinking into the green gloom with me
on his retina. And they never found him.

Five hundred miles inland
all I can think of is the sea.
It's a sea-wind that lifts and drops
the shirt drying at the window.
Our fight has left me reeling.
From the bathroom comes the dribble
and spatter of the shower, feeble
as a ship's faucet. My wife
is in there murmuring a curse
that echoes off the tiled walls.
How did it get like this, she wails.
She stands in a towel at the door.
She is pale as shell. Sobs rake her
like breakers through shingle.
In the street peasants bring cilantro
and peppers from the hills,
stallholders fry tripe and saltado.
By our door a lily wilts in its bottle,
a spent flare. We're too far out,
too far from home.

THE SUMMER OF SPITZ

I think about girls to pass the time –
a different one at each end of the pool.
Mark Spitz

We watched in silence as his shoulders rose
like a pair of brown dolphins from the blue
water, gleaming, spray showering off them.

Behind his black moustache, his sleek brow,
his head was full of girls. Length after length:
girls with blond hair, dark hair, red hair,

small girls, tall girls, curvy girls. Australian,
Californian girls, French and Austrian,
girls from Gambia, girls from Gabon.

We weren't surprised when one after another
the medals fell. Freestyle, butterfly, 100, 200,
relay, medley: only one silver, the rest gold.

He celebrated each girl with a flip-turn
then lunged towards the next.
And we knew he'd never let us down.

THE SPRING

Making a sieve of your fingers you could part
the cress, open the clear water. Motes lifted
and dropped on the faintest current.
Silt folded over itself on the bed, billowing,
a tiny turning cloud. That was the source.
It was the sweetest water. We lowered a jug,
let a trickle spill over the rim, then watched
as my uncle poured a drop that misted his whisky.
It spread through the spirit in lines fine as hair,
in filaments of glass, vanished, and he took a sip.

THE DEEP

The net came up like crumpled silver foil
from the black geometry of the night seas.
A shark lay across the ball of fish. *Fuck*,
muttered the captain. I kept the donkey engine
whining as the boat stooped to meet the weight.
We broke it down, picked through the mesh to the plait
of knots, released the belly-purge, filled the deck
to our ankles in coley, bluefish, monk and haddock.
Only the shark hung still in the sleeve of net,
stiffened into a curve, caught by fin and snout.
The skipper picked up a knife, cut clean
through the cartilage of tail, through blue-grey skin
to snow-white flesh. It swung down with a slap
and slid to the stern, trailing a shiny rope
of gut, with its head half off.

THE PLOT

The three of us sat under the green awning.
Rain clattered overhead, gusted
round our ankles, while the hills flickered
and lightning bolted into the trees.
You told us the plot. The American student
fell in love with the Cuban revolutionary,
her senior, a *barbudo*, who cocktailed her
in Havana's new air. When his plane
crashed in the mountains of Guantanamo
she came home and married the Boston banker
who turned out the light to make love.
Two decades on, she met the revolutionary's brother,
left her sons and husband, ran off
with him to the Hyatt then Mexico.
A month later, dumped, her hands shaking
in a Connecticut hotel room,
her mind unravelled in the New England woods.
She died in a storm of pills.
It was a sad story, a tragedy.
You didn't let on, but we guessed
she was your mother, as you talked on
through the strokes of brilliance
flashing around us, through the roar
that drummed and broke over the hills.

BATTLE OF THE AIR

The propellers had a hole where you put the dab
of glue, then fitted them to the engine snouts:
one, two, three, there they were, the four black fans
of the Avro Lancaster, the Hurricane's single screw.

My brother was the expert. With a teaspoon he opened
tins of paint the size of cotton reels: a meniscus glistened
over cream. Charcoal grey, field brown, fell khaki,
he let the English landscape take over the plane.

It was always Battle of Britain: Spitfire and Blenheim,
planes whose throaty hum we heard as we held them
under the anglepoise. We smoothed their transfers
with the end of a brush, and hung them from loops of thread.

At night we swept the ceiling with torch-beams,
saw the shadows bulge and shift. Bullets sparked
as squadrons peeled one by one onto Messerschmidts
stealing up the Thames, sent them howling into the net of hedges.

And only a few years on we stuffed them with caps,
doused lighter-fuel and jostled for space
at the window to watch them drop to the lawn,
trailing black smoke, and glue themselves to the ground.

The wind took our eyeballs
in its hands and polished them
so we could see properly.
Schools of mackerel were swimming
through the fields, bellies flashing.
We waded among a million
halogen bulbs on green stalks.
Boats were windfalls littering
the estuary. Sunlight grated the water.
On a steep field a flock
of silver sheep cantered uphill.
Or was it an untrimmed sail?
Whatever. We returned to the village's lee
and oiled our wind-dry minds
with dark bottles, heavy bubbling casseroles.
The sun cracked like an egg on the roof,
spilling down the windows.

SUNDAY

Let's talk about today, how we drove
across a simple land, land of an easier time,
past fogbound trees, among alloyed affluence.
Neither of us knew how much hope
the other held, but we'd been listening
to Miles Davis, he set an easy Sunday tone.
Lunch at a bistro, rosemary lamb,
Mediterranean vegetables, that kind of thing,
and all the time me trying to stay in touch
with that relaxed feeling, keep out of panic.
A walk in the park where I walked as a kid –
same trees, same river, same pond with ducks –
a pleasant walk, but me thinking: why
isn't this enough, in fact it *is* enough,
to expect more is a ticket to misery.
A frieze of orange marble lit up the sky.
Then driving home past ghostly hills
and blurred trees I turned to your profile,
watched you watching the headlights emerge
from the night, and thought: where do they
come from, we think we know but we don't.
On we raced through the black land,
black world, behind our own pair of stars,
imagining we knew where we were going.

BADGER

We worked at night in Paul's garage under
a bare bulb, me on my Puch, he on his Triumph.
From his cartridge deck pedal-steel twanged,
Tammy and George wailed in the rafters.
He called me Badger, I never knew why.

Come on, Badger, pass the emery. We filed the needle
so my carburettor wouldn't stick, unsheathed
the growling baffles. The exhaust hung like a weapon
to the undercarriage, pouring blue smoke. We stripped
the tank to a bulb of chrome, lost the headlamp,

and one Saturday night he shoved me off the stand.
I dropped the starter, gravel spattered and I felt
the sure line the front wheel drew when riding on power.
Lightless, lidless, I hurtled out the gate, the wheels
juddering on frosty tarmac. I came to at the first bend

in the ditch, drenched, cold, a sweet pain
singing in wrist and shoulder. The rich smell
of two-stroke on the verge, one wheel ticking.
The engine gasped. My eyes burned and I heard
the thud of boots as Paul came running down the hill.

TRUMPETERS

Dad keeps his old trumpet in the cupboard.
The frayed leather case smells of dust.
The clips clunk, he lifts the lid. Inside,
the gold bell rests on its bed of velvet.
He wipes the gleaming tubes, sluices oil
in the valves, flicks them wheezing
on their springs. Tries a bar of *Ain't Misbehavin'*.

Humphrey did that. He peers at me over the bell.
Played with him once. Years ago, of course.
He can't help smiling as his cheeks inflate.
Play along, boychick, we're in C. I don't know
what to do, blow a bottom C on my rented
Boosey, then a G, while he splits his tune.
Better use the mutes, Helen's downstairs.

Rain plays a light snare on the skylight, leaves
stick to the glass, beyond them the sky is purple,
dark already at five. Out come the music cards,
the Salvation Army lyres with little brass screws.
We attempt *Away in a Manger, Once in Royal*.
In three weeks we'll be out, he and I, a carol duet
buttoned in our coats under a street lamp, fingers freezing.

I'll pay you to go away, a neighbour will cry,
half-joking. Dad will laugh into his instrument,
making it screech. For now in the yellow light
of his desk lamp we settle *While Shepherds Watched*
in the clips, press our lips against the mouthpieces,
against our muted harmony, as long as we can,
until downstairs calls and we put the trumpets away.

Marie's got stuck on repeaters today.
Knees up! Knees up! Our benches groan.
She moves like a cat just ahead of the beat,
ponytail tapping either shoulder blade.
She's taken off her shirt, down to Batman bra,
lycra shorts. A blue tattoo peeps over the hem.
What is it? A dolphin? A spider? *OK!* she shouts.
March it out! Her buttocks flex. *Basic left!*
Turn–turn, thud–thud, turn–turn, thud. *Arms!*
Up they go, braced for imaginary weights.
The fat guy hates the butterfly arms, does them
halfway. We *glute-squeeze*, we *abductor*,
we *travel-straddle*, we *round-the-world-and-kick*,
we *up-and-lunge*, *power-lunge*, *double-lunge*.
Miss Latina with the gun–barrel eyes gets me
in her sights in the mirror. Caught me eyeing her.
Marie's spine bends desirably as she ballerina-kicks.
My sneakers turn to clay, my shirt drips
and clings. Not Marie – dry as a bone.
Take a pulse, warm-down time. That tattoo –
a butterfly, a bat? An orchid? It's stretches now.
I can see the mound between her legs.
Back-rolls! Marie's light and young,
strong and hard, everything I want to be.
Come on, let's back-roll together, you and me.
The boxer in the gallery quits thumping his bag,
peers down, gloves dangling over the rail.
The raquetball players glance from the door
as the class groans and gasps like a rusty machine,
grins on every face now because it's *big-inhale*
time, *grab-some-water* time. We sigh, we clap
ourselves as Marie marches it out once more.

She tweaks her shorts, peels back the hem
like a fruit rind, smiles over her shoulder,
and there it is, branded on her rump: an open fig.

It was always Clarks. Brown sandals
with aerated uppers, black lace-ups
with metal rings round the eyelets,
slip-ons with V's of elastic and such smooth
soles you could do a skid on the pavement,
and they'd slide clean off your bike pedal.
The silver-haired woman peered down
as you sat on the stool with the padded ramp.
She took your heel in her fingers,
jammed it in the measuring stirrup.
Down came the toecap on its runners,
pressing till she got the reading.
Looks like six double-E, or five and a half F.
Let's strap him in to make sure.
You'd sit shoeless, waiting till she reappeared
balancing boxes. She'd unravel tissue paper,
pull out a gleaming boat of leather,
fragrant and hard. *Not bad, have a walk.*
You'd slap down the store already feeling
the edge that would cut your heel in coming weeks.
She'd press the toe with her bony thumb.
Yes, plenty of space. I'm not sure, you'd try,
I think it hurts at the back. *It'll loosen up.*
And that was it, you'd be clopping flat-footed
downstairs, along the road, reminded wherever
you went that a new term was on its way,
a new winter, another bandage on the heel.

POTOMAC MOTEL

It's three a.m., my chances are running out.
If I don't act soon, she'll leave me
to the white ocean of my expense account.
I watch her settle in the chair with a filled flute.
Screw that boyfriend of yours, I think.
Or rather don't. Stay. I can tell by her smile
she's not averse. *Woodstock* is on TV,
Hendrix ravishing the Stars and Stripes.
Maybe he'll get her in the mood.
Do you know how beautiful you are, I try.
She smiles that smile again.
Outside, the river sails past with its freight
of lights. She drains her glass and gets up,
says, Right. One hug and she's gone.
I can't resist the remote. Tattooed breasts,
Titanic nipples. Shining orbs, milky comets
sprung by young hands. One is pretty,
looks like her. I have to switch off.
I light a cigarette and listen to cars
droning down the parkway. Next door
the creaking of bedsprings, a murmur of voices.

LEAVING

A last wade through the fields. Home
comes up to your waist. I know this view:
the camouflage of woods,
a single plane crawling into evening.

My wife, who doesn't want to leave,
takes solace in a tub under that red roof,
longing for a mutual longing – a cottage
sunk in grey hills, an oceanic window.

The larks are going crazy.
Swallows skim the grass like fish.
A train sighs to Oxford, unseen,
and the grass hisses, *stay, stay.*

THE TAXI DRIVER

The door yelped on its hinge. Time was tight,
this was not the cab I needed: an old sedan,
its upholstery sagging onto the chassis.
He took downtown at a stately pace, losing three greens.

Out on the freeway he swooped to the exit lane
with a whistle: *Almost forgot the gas.*
At the Chevron station smoke billowed from the hood.
There goes my flight, I thought. *Just a little oil I spilled.*

He moved gently, precisely as a cat across the forecourt
to pay. He had a belly, wore big shades.
Hurry up, I hissed, as a jet cruised overhead.
I'll leave you to your thoughts, he said, smiling in the mirror.

Maybe it was the sunny afternoon, the chalky
windows, the luxury of ancient suspension,
or the man's calm bulk in front of me, but I felt better.
We traded origins. He was Menominee from Wisconsin.

His tidy, *piano* voice was pleasant on the ear.
A hot air balloon hung on the horizon, prompted him
about a tribal fast on the Continental Divide when a balloon
came over. He hollered from the trees, saw the people

peering down, trying to figure where he was.
They landed, gave him the last of their champagne.
Hey, look at this gift of the white people, he told
his companions. None of them could touch it.

At the airport he plucked my bags from the oily trunk,
turned to me, opened his arms and pulled me in.
He was warm, soft, damp. I could hardly find the eyes
in those broad cheeks, but when I did they shone at me.

At passport control I thought of him high in the Colorado
sunshine, holding out a green bottle with an inch left.
As I hurried on I wished I'd taken his card, wished a lot
of things. There was still time for a coffee at the gate.

STORM LINES

The storm has the lane rippling and smoking.
The sky has come apart, scuds by in pieces.
Telephone wires belly between their poles.
In the distance a hill, in its lee must be the river
shivering in these winds, the fields of ripped hay.
In the refuge of a dazzling phone box
I dial an old number down the cracking lines.
Operator, put me through. *We have no record.*
But the house must still be there, and the fields
swarmed by winds, the trees bent double. The sky
warps and sings like a saw. This must be the way.

SPRING LAMB

A filthy rag in the straw: the ewe
licks it but it won't budge. She turns away
on those thin, close-together legs
like a wading bird, birth-strings dangling.

But the little heap, wet mop, discovers
its bleat – a moan – and a twitch, a buck.
It puts out a leg like a walking-stick.
Up, bent-kneed, keeling, collapsing.

Then up again, all four pegs pegged out,
hull held clear on its spider-paws,
and it disappears, tail flicking,
under the mother's dirty fringe.

CROW HILL

At first I thought it was an aviary for a hawk.
But a chicken-wire funnel led into it,
and weather-grey skulls littered the floor
and ribs of sheep picked clean: a trap.

My approach agitated the birds inside.
They bounced back and forth without a sound.
Hooded crows, three of them. Gangly, grey,
almost topheavy with those monomaniac beaks.

And guilty, or shameless, like bullies who'd never
hear sense, you couldn't ask them to lay off your lambs.
The birds were doomed, you could feel it.
I waited for them to settle but they wouldn't.

They turned away, not wanting to see me.
Out in the field a raven's wing spread over
a mess of down which the sun, on the brink
of a mountainous cloud, made white as snow.

TRAIN ROBBERS

We each put an ear to the rail Indian-style,
heard a hiss, an electric twang. A churn of engine
bounced off a hill — a tractor dawdling, a plane
crawling across the sky? The singing in the rails

began to seethe, ricochet from line to line: a hollow
knocking of mallets. Which way? Our pennies
and spoons lay taped to the ribbon where the iron
had worn to a shine. A horn stabbed a warning.

Which way? Drums clattered round our ears. There it was,
a thundering diesel, yellow face greased with mud,
its coaltrucks bulking round the bend of trees
like hurtling houses. Afterwards we searched the sleepers,

spotted a glint in the hardcore, a silver coin
thin as a leaf, all trace of its minting gone.
The spoons flattened into lollipops
you'd have cut your tongue on, hot to the touch.

DENTISTS

First, Mr Sharpe of Herne Road: the afternoon
heavy as mercury in his waiting room,
with its furtive throat-clearings, cracklings
of old *Country Life*s. He came beaming
out of his corner like a miner, an Inca.
The drill fizzed and whined against my bones,
and I cried to the blind eye on his forehead.
Later, he made a plaster model of my jaws:
there they sat, grinning on his metal tray.

Then the modern type – NASA pyjamas,
face mask, white slippers, Mercedes outside –
who talked like an uncle. *How's work, my friend?*
He tutted, shook his head. *You haven't flossed.*
His spooky dinosaur hissed, craned a six-foot neck
to peer into my mouth with two luminous eyes.

Now Janice, of suntanned cleavage,
pornographic voice. *Naughty boy, smoking still?*
Her professional hands tackle the instruments
of hygiene. The farce begins, the gurgles,
whizzes, sucks, as the stiff white package
of her chest descends. I imagine unbuttoning it,
but she's at me with the pick. Her spotlight
hurts my teeth, and I stare so hard
at the ceiling-rose that everything starts to shine.

The pollen soup of evening wind buffeted
your eyelids till they wept. The pores threw out
hives so fast they came up white and springy
like mushrooms. At night your fingers bloated
and the hours of rubbing commenced: wrist
against corrugated cuff, ankle against heel,
heel ankle, backs of fingers interlocked
like crimping irons, rubbing till they bled.
You'd wrap each finger in a coil of sheet,
let the ripped parts seep, soaking the cloth.
Aureomycin, yellow and oily, Graneodin,
Tri-Adcortyl – the creams were all useless.
Tubs of E45 and Aqueous B.P., Coal-Tar Paste
and Oilatum only made the sores itch and run.
Coal-Tar Bandages went on, grey and cool
from the fridge, building a hide as thick
as a rhino's. Next day it had to be cracked off,
left the fingers red and raw, unused to air.
Doctor Vicars said you'd grow out of it. *Top
of the form? See, you make up for it in other ways.*
The woman in jersey and beads held your palms,
gave you little white pills and tincture of marigold
in brown bottles. Your hands seethed. *Good,*
she said, *well done. Look at it coming out.*
Bubbles clustered under the skin, lymph poured,
turned overnight to orange crystal, flakes of ash.
Porridge-Face. The Thing from Doctor Who.
A continent of crimson etched itself up each arm.
The doctor called it third degree, sent you to hospital
where you lay in stiff sheets while a young consultant
spread cool cream over the red crazy paving.
We don't like to use a powerful steroid, he said,
unless we have to. The skin drank it in.

The crevasses closed, the scrublands became smooth.
Soon your fingers were unblemished
as a fresh snowfield, as those perfect sheets.

NEW YEAR TRAIN

Our train grumbles through suburban night.
Orange stars wheel by, ghosts in the window
down cans of lager. There'll be parties later.

I read a poem by a man from long ago
in which that man, one slushy November,
reads poems by a man from long ago.

He called it dark winter, the eleventh month:
a time for looking back. Here on the train
the year is done. I think back; November:

the year is a house, and November is a quiet room.
One should sit at a desk and watch rain fall
on a lawn. I was busy. My life is full

of missed Novembers: the cottage I left,
the flat I could have stayed in – if only
I hadn't moved, had settled, it would have done fine.

Better than anything since. I don't mind exactly.
There's comfort in an imperfect present,
in knowing we can be less than we might be.

And am I not just approaching the year's fence,
preparing to barrow dead leaves against it?
The train gathers itself in a rattle of triumph

as if moving towards something that will really happen.
Station by station we desert it,
and it travels faster, lighter into the night.

AFTER THE RADIOLOGY

Driving home from the hospital,
you say, *Those clouds have a gold lining.*

I look up, and it's true,
but I don't want to think about it.

Instead I see myself going to the shops
and coming home too late;

or waking beside you one morning
and thinking you're asleep.

I want to be with you in this, but I'm not:
if I lose you you lose more.

Tomorrow we'll know everything,
you say, and turn to me with a smile.

It wus never a flud, they got it all rong.
It wus a heetwave. Who ever herd of a flud
in the desert? As if we wud hav minded.
We didnt pich up on that peek to keep dry
but cool. You cant imagin the heet.
It rold in like invisibal fire, like lions breth.
Never mind an eg you cud fry a stake
on a rok, and in the shade. Sandals smoked
with every step. You had to wair 2 pairs
and even then run. Sleeping – a nitemare,
a joke. The only way to lie down wus to souse
yor bed evry our with water – warm water –
if you cud find it. Who wonts to shlep
to the well and bak 6 times a nite?
For shlep I meen skip. Forget dreems.
Dreems evaporated before they cud reech us.

We took to a cave. It wus cool as a buchers
at ferst. Cudnt beleev our luk, problem solvd,
wed wate it out. We hung blankits over the mouth
to keep out the sun. Then dusnt the erth
heet up round us like an uven. The place ternd
into a bakers. The animals started showing up,
limping, wining. The lions came ferst and purd
at the blankits. I let them in. The lady nuzzeld
my elbow, likt my hand with that scraper-
tung of hers. She drew blud but didnt meen to
and never came bak for mor. They straggeld
past our pots and rugs, curld up in the caves dark.
After that we cud hardly refuse the rest.

In they cum, 2 by 2 trew enuff.
Grunts, grumbels, grones. Mones and mews,

wines and wimpers. Cluks, chirrups,
werrings, buzzes, wissals, flooting.
Piping, worbling, fluttring, droning.
Berps, farts, sies – you name it we herd it.
The cave fild with the gurgels of a milion
animal slumbers. Youd think it wudve stunk
but the mingeld odors of a milion beests
wer sweet to the nostral like a bloom of flours.
And the dung? Strange but there wus nun.

The sky ternd yellow. We stopt eeting.
The apitite dusnt do well at that heet.
We neither slept nor woke. Ime no hero
but sumthing had to be dun. So I organize
the boys. We lit a fire outside, wated til
the coles glowed then herded the lot strate out
onto them. The trik is wuns theyve been over
those coles the ground dusnt seem so hot.
A quik shok and you can handel enything.
Shem led the way: up the hill as fast
as we cud. A din of bleetings and bellows
such as never herd before, up we gallop,
drumming that smoking ground – a caravan
of ansesters herling it self up the mountin.

We capt the peek up there like a nippal.
It wusnt exactly cool but we had a chance.
The sky wus blew agen for 1 thing.
Down below all you cud see wus yellow fog.
No ground, no hills. We hung on our iland of air.
So cleer up there, cleer as a shaving mirrer.
You hav a good long look at yorself
at a time like that. I didn't like wot I saw:
greed and mor greed. Iternal disatisfaction.
Therst does funny things to you.

I even wept. I had no teers of corse
but I felt the rivulets of dust on my cheek
like guttermarks on brik. I felt rite to weep.

Its trew a duv flew up to us. A spek
shivring in the haze below, it flapt it self
into shape like a mirage cuming up
from the fog. It lit on my sholder,
put its beek to my eer to wisper sumthing –
the sweetest messige ever herd.
Tho I cudnt make it out at ferst,
not until I put my finger in my eer.
I drew it out cool: a drop of water
bellying on the end of it. I tried to shout
the news but my throte wudnt make a sound.

The ferst drops steemd, sizzeld and stung.
By then I didn't no if any 1 in the sprall
of flesh wus alive still. But as the rain fell
I herd mones and yelps all round, a crazy
dog barkt up at the thunderheds
in a rage, a fox howled, the frogs flooted
like an organ. Neks rose like plant stems.
Wite clouds bloomd up from the yellow fog.
I cried wen I saw them. I new we had wun.
Thats the trooth. I never got my voice bak
so I cudnt put rite the talk of fluds.
Not until I lernt pen and ink. And I wus
sixty when it happend not 6 hundred.
If I liv to 2 hundred Ile be happy. A drop
just fell on my page. I luv the rain, who dusnt.
Anuther drop. Like littal berrees, spattrings
of juce wair they hit my ink. I let them be.
Be the teers I cudnt cry. The Lords dew.